Where is Major?

by Venita Kaye Bolden and Dr. Wilner Bolden, III

Illustrated by Chermel Bluitt

ACKNOWLEDGMENTS:

This book is dedicated to
my grandmother, Hazel Mae Phillips,
who taught me the importance of independence
and having an excellent prayer life,
and my mother-in-law, Annie Reed,
who has been there supporting
and cheering me on from the beginning.

Copyright©2021 by Venita Kaye Bolden & Dr. Wilner Bolden, III
All rights reserved.
No part of this book/publication may be used or reproduced, stored in a retrieval system, or transmitted in any form or by any means, electronic, mechanical, photocopying, recording, or otherwise, without written permission of the publisher.

ISBN- 978-1-7353265-1-1

Thank you for buying an authorized edition of this book and for complying with copyrights laws by not reproducing, scanning, or distributing and part of it in any form without permission.

For information/Permission Contact:
boldenchildrenbooks@gmail.com

Publish July 2021

Where is Major?

Venita Kaye Bolden and Dr. Wilner Bolden, III

Illustrated by Chermel Bluitt

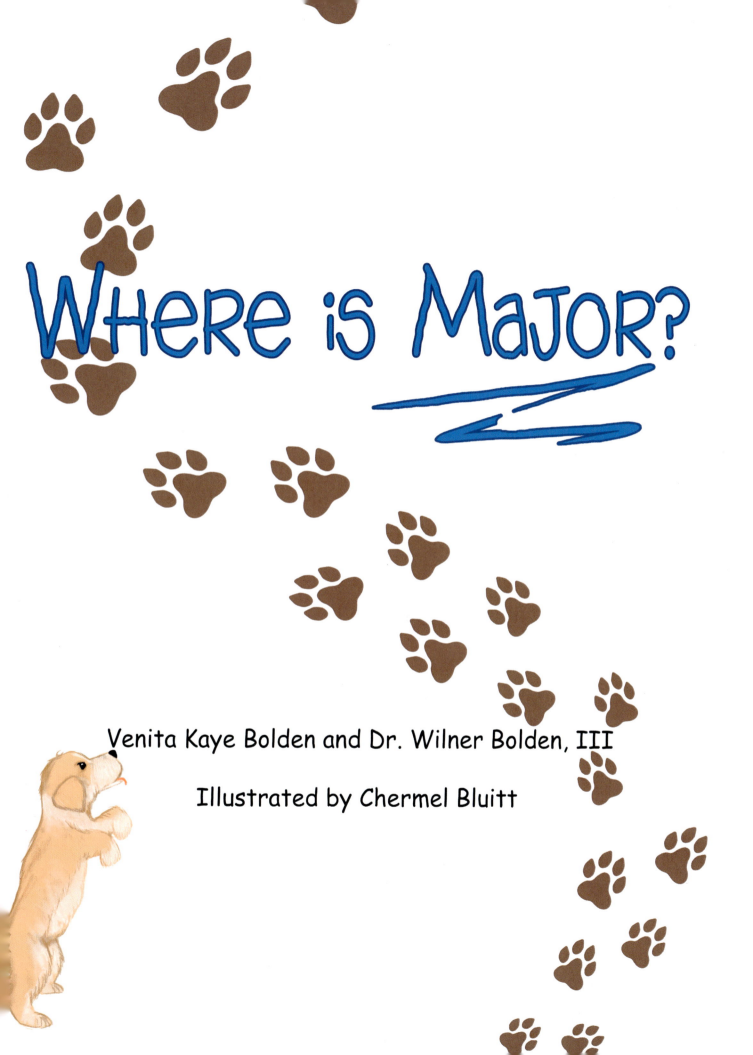

School was out, and Rusty was riding the bus home. During the bus ride, he would share stories with his bus driver, Ms. Annie, about his dog, Major.

"I cannot wait to play with my best friend," said Rusty.

"Well, you will get the chance because this is your stop," replied Ms. Annie. "Say hi to Major for me."

Rusty walked off the school bus and ran into the house.

"Major!" yelled Rusty, "I am home!"

But there was no sound.

"Where is my dog?" said Rusty. "Why doesn't he answer me?"

Rusty ran into the living room where his grandfather was reading the newspaper.

"Grandfather, have you seen Major?" asked Rusty.

"No, but I am sure he is somewhere hiding," replied Grandfather.

Rusty yelled again, "Major, where are you?"

Again, there was no Major.

"Maybe Grandfather is right. Major is probably hiding."

Rusty decided to look for his dog.

"Where could he be? Maybe he is in the bedroom hiding from me."

Rusty looked in his bedroom.
He looked inside the closet.
He looked under his orange pillow.
He looked under his blue bed.
Can you guess what he found?
Rusty found a round nickel; it was right there under his bed.

"Where is Major? Where could he be? Maybe he is in the kitchen hiding from me."

Rusty looked in the kitchen.
He looked in the pantry.
He looked inside the grey sink.
He looked under the red table
and black chairs.
Can you guess what he found?
Rusty found a dime and a penny on the floor
under the chairs.

"Where is Major? Where could he be? Maybe he is in the bathroom hiding from me."

Rusty looked in the bathroom.
He looked inside the shower.
He looked in the white tub.
He looked in the brown cabinet.
Can you guess what he found?
Rusty found a shiny quarter in the cabinet on the bottom shelf.

"Where is Major? Where could he be? Maybe he is in the living room hiding from me."

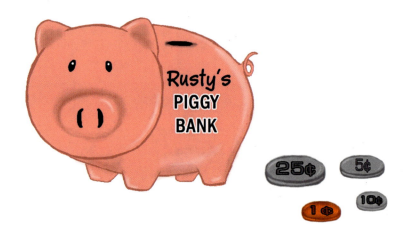

Rusty looked in the living room.
He looked behind the couch.
He looked behind the green chair.
He looked under the yellow sofa.
Can you guess what he found?
Rusty found a dollar under the big sofa next to the chair.

"Where is Major? Where could he be? Maybe he is outside hiding from me."

Rusty looked outside.
He looked in the backyard
near the red slide.
He looked in the front yard
near the green bushes.
He looked in the doghouse
and behind the tree.
Can you guess what he found?
Rusty found two dollars laying at the foot
of the tree.

Rusty ran back into the house crying, "Where
are you, Major?"

He sat on the living room floor and began to cry.

Suddenly, Rusty heard a noise at the front door!

"Rusty, we are home!" shouted his grandmother.

Rusty heard Major barking with glee! He jumped to his feet with excitement, ran to Major, and hugged his neck.

"Major, I thought I lost you!" yelled Rusty.

"Grandmother, where were you and Major?"

"I took him to the vet for his annual checkup," she replied. "He is in good health, and you both will be best friends for a long time!"

"Major, did you hear that? We will be best friends for a long time!"

"Major, I love you! Now let's count the money I found."